Demand and Supply: Learning from the Un

Jason Furman
Chairman, Council of Economic Advisers

ESRI International Conference 2016
Tokyo, Japan
August 2, 2016

This is an expanded version of these remarks as prepared for delivery.

It is now nearly nine years since the onset of the financial crisis. The world economy is growing, and the advanced economies have made significant progress in recovering, but this healing process has been uneven. Demand shortfalls remain across most advanced economies, as evidenced by very low interest rates and wage and price inflation, as well as unusually high unemployment rates in some European countries and some continued labor market slack elsewhere. Moreover, there are issues with the composition and sources of demand and its resilience in the face of potential future shocks. Longer-run supply challenges, in the form of lower productivity and investment growth, have also been pervasive across all of the advanced economies. This slowdown, together with longer-run trends in demography, rising inequality, and, in some cases, falling labor force participation, has created obstacles for the typical family to see adequate income growth and at the same time has heightened long-run fiscal pressures.

The Obama and Abe Administrations have both focused on vigorous steps that are needed to strengthen economic growth. Challenges on both the demand and supply sides are present in most of the advanced economies and are, in many ways, interrelated. Even if specific circumstances and appropriate policy responses vary from country to country, we have a large number of tools at our disposal to deal with these issues today. That is why it is so important that the G-7 Finance Ministers declared in their May Ise Shima communiqué that:

> "Global growth is our urgent priority…We reiterate our commitments to using all policy tools— monetary, fiscal and structural—individually and collectively, to strengthen global demand and address supply constraints…We reaffirm the important role of mutually-reinforcing fiscal, monetary and structural policies, the three pronged approach, to buttress our efforts to achieve strong, sustainable, and balanced growth."

Since the global financial crisis, the United States and Japan have both used various combinations of fiscal and monetary measures to stimulate growth by boosting demand. Although both political and economic factors have at times constrained our ability to make use of macroeconomic tools, we are also both hard at work fulfilling another part of the plan expressed within the same statement from Ise Shima:

> "We are committed to advancing structural reforms to boost growth, productivity and potential output and to leading by example in addressing structural challenges. We commit to further investment in areas conducive to economic

growth, such as environment, energy, digital economy, human resource development, education, science and technology."

In my remarks today, I will start by discussing the recovery in the advanced economies, focusing especially on the fiscal-policy experiences of the United States, Japan, and Europe. I will then go on to discuss two major structural issues: productivity and labor force participation. One issue that is especially important for the United States but is beyond the scope of my comments today is inequality, including its links to economic rents, which I have addressed elsewhere (CEA 2016a; Furman and Orszag 2015). It is important to note that this is an area where Japan has fared far better than the United States: while the share of income going to the top one percent of households in each country was comparable in 1975, Japan's has risen only slightly, while that of the United States has more than doubled, according to the most recently available data (WWID 2016).

My argument will be that demand, productivity, and participation are related: the magnitude and composition of short-run demand can affect the supply side, including productivity and the labor force. At the same time, productivity and the labor force can themselves affect one another. Global conditions affect long-run equilibrium interest rates; technological progress is not entirely in our hands; and birth rates from past decades affect the size of the population in the future. But none of these changes represent our destiny, and rather than debating whether we are in an era of secular stagnation or lower productivity growth for the long term, the relevant question for policymakers is what we can do about it. And in that regard, I think the United States and Japan have much to learn from each other's successes and challenges—both through more economic research like that discussed in today's conference, as well as through policymakers sharing views with one another.

In both of our cases, responsible fiscal policy will continue to play an important role in generating additional demand. And in both of our cases, structural reforms are needed to increase productivity growth and enhance firm dynamism. Though the exact nature of needed structural reform differs between our countries, one objective we have in common is the Trans-Pacific Partnership (TPP), which is a critical measure to expand trade and encourage faster productivity growth and greater innovation.

Finally, demography may create headwinds and challenges, but by learning from each other about how to enable a larger fraction of the population to work, while ensuring a high-quality environment of care and learning for the next generation, the United States and Japan can both successfully manage our respective demographic challenges.

Divergent Recoveries from the Economic Crises

Growth in the advanced economies picked up in 2014 and 2015 but has still fallen well below the International Monetary Fund's (IMF's) forecasts every year since 2010, as shown in Figure 1. In July, the IMF revised its forecast of near-term growth down further in part as a result of increased global uncertainty due to British voters' decision in June to leave the European Union (IMF 2016b).

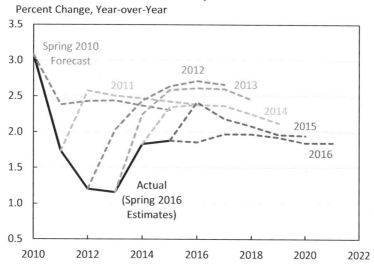

Figure 1
IMF Advanced Economy Real GDP Forecast

Percent Change, Year-over-Year

While all of the advanced economies have faced headwinds, their different challenges and different responses have left them with divergent outcomes— as shown in Figure 2. The United States has made the most progress in terms of per capita GDP. Japan also recovered relatively early—thanks in part to an aggressive fiscal response undertaken with foresight, even though its own banks fared much better than those in some other advanced economies—but has seen its growth rate slip, and while Europe's economy has improved over the last two years, it is on the verge of a missing decade of growth.

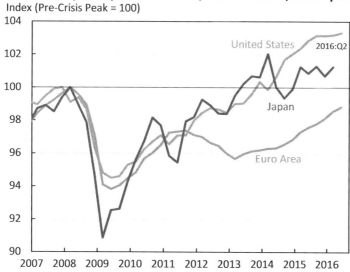

Figure 2
Real GDP per Capita: Euro Area, United States, and Japan

Index (Pre-Crisis Peak = 100)

These output patterns roughly correspond to the evolution of unemployment rates (shown in Figure 3), which have returned to pre-crisis rates in the United States and Japan but remain substantially elevated in the euro area.

Figure 3
Unemployment Rate

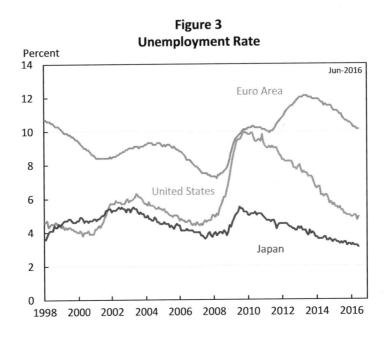

In the United States, per-capita GDP reached a peak at the end of 2007 before falling 5.5 percent in the midst of the worst economic crisis since the Great Depression. In many ways, the shock that precipitated this crisis was even worse than the Great Depression: 19 percent of wealth was wiped out in the first year of the crisis, about five times the amount that was lost in the first year of the Depression, and global trade volumes fell by 19 percent, even more than at the Depression's onset (Furman 2015). By the fourth quarter of 2013, per-capita GDP had recovered to pre-crisis levels, and in the second quarter of this year was 3 percent above its pre-crisis peak. The unemployment rate today is 4.9 percent, below its pre-recession average, and real wages are rising. Overall, the current U.S. economic recovery has outpaced both recoveries from earlier financial crises in the United States and the recent experience of many other countries—in part because of a combination of a large initial fiscal expansion, consistently vigorous monetary policy, and an aggressive financial accounting and clean-up.

Japan's financial sector did not face the same type of crisis, but the country was affected even more by the collapse in global trade and suffered an even larger reduction in output during the crisis than the United States, with per-capita GDP down 9.1 percent from peak to trough (as compared to 5.5 percent for the United States). Coming after more than a decade of low growth and low inflation, the global crisis posed unique challenges for any potential monetary response. Consequently, Japan undertook a number of aggressive fiscal measures—some of the most aggressive discretionary fiscal stimulus among advanced economies—which helped put per-capita output back on the same track as the United States and well ahead of the euro area. However, a range of factors—including the 2011 earthquake and tsunami and the 2014 consumption tax hike—contributed to a "stop-and-go" recovery for Japan, with output generally flat in the last two years. Struggles boosting inflation (shown in Figure 4) above zero are consistent with lingering slack in the economy, the difficulty of re-anchoring inflation

4

expectations, and the fragility of domestic demand. To the degree that inflation follows expectations and expectations are linked to past inflation, re-anchoring inflation presents a particular challenge on the heels of about two decades of actual inflation more often than not has hovered near or dipped below zero.

Figure 4
Core Inflation

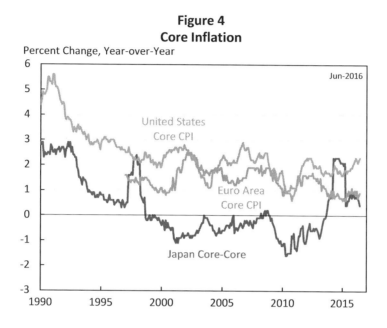

In addition, despite Japan enjoying the lowest unemployment rate it has had in twenty years, a fuller picture of the labor market is also indicative of slack in the economy. In Japan, changes in output are associated with much smaller changes in unemployment than in other advanced economies. This is because the formal labor market makes it relatively hard to fire workers while the large role of bonuses in labor compensation makes it relatively easy to adjust nominal wages down. As a result, in downturns firms tend to hoard labor, cut wages, and cut hours—while the opposite happens in expansions. In the current expansion, however, hours in Japan have not recovered in the same way that employment has, as shown in Figure 5. This may help explain the lack of substantial wage inflation despite low unemployment and high ratios of job openings to job seekers.

Figure 5
Japan: Real GDP, Employment, and Hours Worked

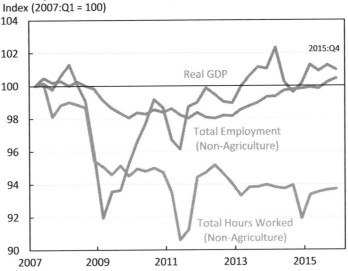

The euro area is growing at about the same pace as the United States and faster than Japan, with a falling unemployment rate, but per-capita GDP is still more than 1 percent below its pre-crisis peak. According to medium-term projections by the IMF, the euro area will have suffered through nearly a decade of lost economic growth. Moreover, although the euro area has long had higher structural unemployment than the United States and especially than Japan, at 10 percent today its unemployment rate is well above any plausible measure of structural unemployment. The labor market has recovered in a few European countries, but not in the region as a whole. As the euro area crisis hit, substantial austerity policies were implemented in a number of countries despite large output gaps and monetary policy at the zero lower bound. A combination of fiscal rules, their interpretation and implementation, and government commitments has precluded significant, deliberate fiscal stimulus measures in many economies and has also led to overly rapid and premature fiscal consolidations. In addition, the European Central Bank was slower to cut interest rates and early in the crisis expanded its balance sheet far less than did the Federal Reserve. The ECB even *raised* rates in 2011. In addition, as the initial stress tests for large banks were not considered credible and financial policy was largely handled at the national—not currency-area—level, financial problems mingled with fiscal problems, hampering growth.

The Role of Fiscal Policy

Monetary, fiscal and financial policies have all played a role in these divergent outcomes. In my discussion today I will focus more on fiscal policy, exploring three of its aspects: (1) the role of fiscal policy in ensuring sufficient aggregate demand; (2) the balance of fiscal and monetary policy; and (3) the question of fiscal space.

The Role of Fiscal Policy In Ensuring Sufficient Aggregate Demand

Between 2009 and 2012, the United States passed more than a dozen expansionary fiscal measures that included a combination of individual tax cuts; business tax incentives; investments in infrastructure, energy, and research; relief for State and local governments; and expanded transfer payments. In total, these measures delivered $1.4 trillion of discretionary fiscal stimulus, or an average of 2 percent of GDP over that four-year period. Together with automatic stabilizers, the total fiscal stimulus averaged 4 percent of GDP over that period. In total, as measured by the change in the primary balance as a share of GDP, the United States had more fiscal stimulus than Japan or the euro area in each year from 2008 to 2010, as shown in Figure 6. Japan ranked second in those years, and then had the largest fiscal impetus thereafter as the amount of stimulus in the United States fell short of what was needed and was withdrawn too soon, contrary to proposals made by President Obama. But nevertheless, the large response helped shape the trajectory of the economy at a critical time.

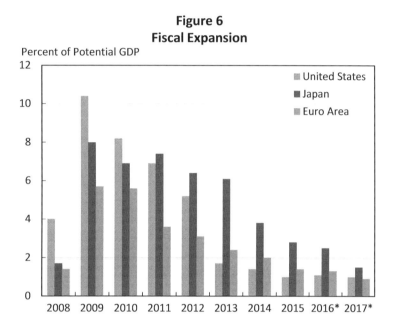

Figure 6
Fiscal Expansion

In 2014, however, the consumption tax rate in Japan was raised from 5 to 8 percent, with VAT revenue increasing by nearly 1 percent as a share of GDP between 2013 and 2014, as shown in Figure 7. This abrupt fiscal contraction contributed to a 2.6-percent fall in per-capita output from which Japan has yet to fully recover. As such, the recent decisions to delay the next consumption tax increase represent a welcome recognition that too much fiscal consolidation too soon can spell trouble for growth. Moreover, the additional stimulus in the Prime Minister's anticipated fiscal package would provide additional support to economic growth. While the details were not available as of preparing these remarks, it remains important to continue to focus on a plan that is both substantial and consistent with the idea of serious, upfront stimulus coupled with sensible, longer-term fiscal consolidation.

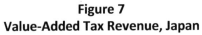

Figure 7
Value-Added Tax Revenue, Japan

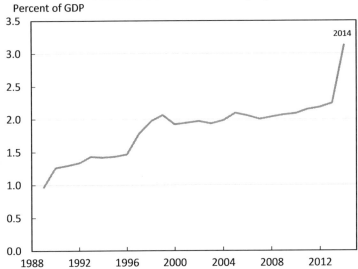

The Appropriate Balance of Fiscal and Monetary Policy

One question is whether the overall magnitude of aggregate demand is sufficient. In the United States, the answer to that question, as evidenced by the unemployment rate and the output gap, is getting closer to "yes"—although there are still areas of slack in both the U.S. and Japanese labor markets. Along with the lack of growth in per-capita GDP and an inflation rate that is well below target, this is consistent with deficient demand. In the euro area, meanwhile, it is clear that demand is deficient and in urgent need of addressing, as indicated by the area's excessive unemployment rate and its output gap.

A second question is the composition of demand, and in particular the relative weight of monetary versus fiscal policy. Many commentators have suggested that in a wide range of advanced economies monetary policy has shouldered a disproportionate share of the burden without sufficient help from fiscal policy. The evidence for this view includes unusually low real interest rates—below even any plausible measure of a new, lower long-run equilibrium rate—across the advanced economies and the fact that inflation is below target in all of the advanced economies.

Moreover, under-reliance on fiscal policy has downsides. An implication of arguments by Gauti Eggertsson, Neil Mehrotra, Sanjay Singh, and Larry Summers (2016) is that in a world characterized by inadequate demand and low interest rates, when monetary policy acts alone, it may simply shift demand between countries rather than adding to total demand, leading to mercantilist outcomes and potentially encouraging protectionism. In such a world, the demand effects in other countries of policies that lead to large current account surpluses cannot be offset, and hence can be problematic. Fiscal policy, on the other hand, can increase demand both in the country that uses it and in other countries as well. In addition, fiscal policy has the potential not just to expand demand today but also to increase supply via investments in infrastructure, addressing the productivity issues I will discuss in a few moments.

Fiscal Space

The downside of fiscal policy is the issue of long-run sustainability—in other words, the question of which countries have fiscal space. In one sense the answer to this question is "all of them," or at least all countries that have credible political systems that are capable of making commitments, since upfront fiscal expansion can be combined with medium- and long-term fiscal consolidation. In the United States, for example, the average annual 2 percent of GDP in fiscal stimulus that was enacted from 2009 through 2012 coincided with three large medium-to-long-term fiscal consolidations: the Affordable Care Act, which included Medicare savings and additional revenue, primarily from high-income households; the Budget Control Act, which put limits on discretionary spending; and the expiration of tax cuts for high-income households at the end of 2012. The combination of these measures with economic and other developments substantially reduced the U.S. fiscal gap (the difference between the present value of projected expenditures and the present value of revenues).

A second question in assessing fiscal space is the debt impact of a policy that raises both the numerator and the denominator of the debt-to-GDP ratio. Recent research has found that in the presence of the effective lower bound on interest rates, fiscal policy, and especially programs geared for long-term payoffs—like increasing incentives for private investment and R&D and public investment in human capital or, in some cases, infrastructure—can optimize welfare, yield high fiscal multipliers, or even expand output sufficiently to result in a reduced debt-to-GDP ratio (DeLong and Summers 2012; Ostry, Ghosh, and Espinoza 2015; IMF 2016a). Research by the OECD suggests that low interest rates have increased fiscal space in the short term and shows how even budget-neutral increases in public investment and education can boost GDP growth (Mourougane et al. 2016) These results do not necessarily mean that these types of long-term investments or other fiscal expansion need never be paid-for, as they depend both on the particular constraints on monetary policy and the way in which expectations about the fiscal situation affect interest rates. But the fact that a range of very different models give similar answers to this question is, at the very least, worth taking seriously.

Third, while not every country has the same degree of fiscal space, the risk today is towards excessive caution. Based on current interest rates, the judgment of capital markets is that borrowing by most countries at this point would be safe, in part because many countries have taken significant steps to reduce their long-run fiscal gaps (Italy's pension reforms, for example). Moreover, the decline in interest rates is not a new phenomenon—real interest rates have been falling since the 1980s in major advanced economies and were already relatively low even before the extraordinary steps taken to combat the crisis, as shown in Figure 8.

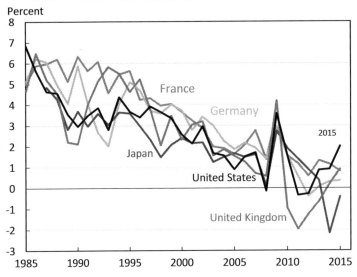

Figure 8
Real 10-Year Benchmark Rate in Selected Countries

Low interest rates have also resulted in relatively low interest payments as a share of GDP. Japan pays 0.3 percent of GDP in net interest on government debt each year, lower than any other G-7 country (as shown in Figure 9). The United States pays 2.8 percent of its GDP in debt interest; other advanced economies are also near historic lows.

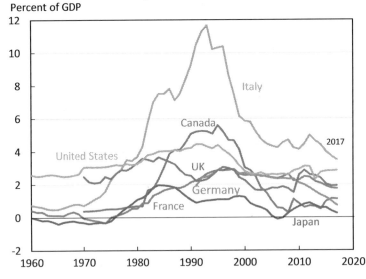

Figure 9
Net Interest Payments on Government Debt

Of course, interest rates are likely below their long-term values and can also shift rapidly in the face of changing circumstances. The forecast underlying the U.S. Federal Budget assumes that the rate on 10-year Treasuries will rise by about 200 basis points over the ten-year forecast window, consistent with private forecasters and the Congressional Budget Office (CBO) and arguably a more conservative assumption than the judgment of financial markets.

In Japan, interest rates on Japanese Government Bonds (JGBs) have long been held down by home bias among investors, a lack of other investment opportunities, and monetary policy that includes ownership of government debt equal to a remarkable 59 percent of total net debt. These factors cannot all necessarily be counted on to the same degree going forward, as there is some evidence for diminished home bias in Japanese savings in addition to the impact that a shrinking and aging population will have on the demand for government bonds. Moreover, with net debt of 130 percent of GDP, Japan is more sensitive than other countries to changes in interest rates.

Arguments about lack of fiscal space and the determinants of market confidence have been overstated in a number of countries. Japan, for example, did not see a spike in interest rates following its two consumption tax delays—in part because these steps were understood to result in higher output and thus potentially an even lower debt-to-GDP ratio. But the risks of upfront actions would be further decreased if they were accompanied by longer-term fiscal consolidations; for example, a number of analysts have suggested putting the consumption tax on a gradual upward path.

Fiscal policy, combined with well-designed structural reforms, can also help address two longer-run challenges to which I will now turn: slowing productivity growth and labor force growth. In both of these cases, policy has a role to play in mitigating some of the adverse pressures created by demographic trends—something that is particularly true for Japan.

Supply and Demand: The Role of Productivity Growth

While there is still substantial heterogeneity across economies in terms of their cyclical position, there is an unfortunate uniformity in terms of their experience with productivity growth. Average annual productivity growth in the advanced economies slowed to less than 1 percent from 2005 to 2015, down from 2 percent in the previous decade—with productivity slowing in 30 of the 31 advanced economies, including all of the G-7 economies, as shown in Figure 10. The United States and Japan have had some of the strongest records in terms of productivity growth in the last decade, but in both cases productivity has slowed substantially relative to the decade before.

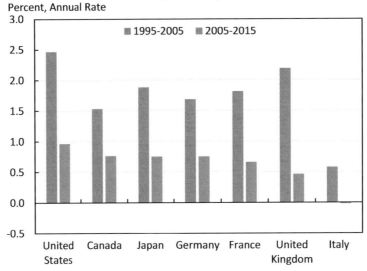

Figure 10
Labor Productivity Growth, G-7 Countries

The Role of Reduced Investment in the Productivity Slowdown: Demand Causes Supply

It is unlikely to be a mere coincidence that a substantial shortfall in aggregate demand and a large slowdown in productivity growth have occurred simultaneously. In fact, the causal relationship between the two phenomena likely runs both ways. Inadequate demand has contributed to a large shortfall of investment, which was 20 percent below the IMF's 2007 forecast in the advanced economies in 2008-2014. As shown in Figure 11, this largely reflects a shortfall of business investment. Japan is notable for having public and residential investment *above* the 2007 IMF forecast; however, these have not offset its far larger shortfall in business investment, which has exceeded the corresponding shortfall in other advanced economies.

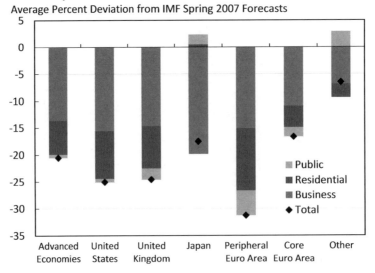

Figure 11
Decomposition of the Investment Slowdown, 2008-2014

In the United States, total factor productivity growth (measured on a five-year moving average basis) is below its historical average, as shown in Figure 12. However, the largest contributor to recent low productivity growth is the decline, for the first time since World War II, in capital services per worker-hour in the last five years—due both to slower investment growth and a large increase in worker hours. As a result, a worker today has *less* capital at his or her disposal than a worker five years ago. Moreover, growth in business investment has continued to slow in recent years, even declining in the fourth quarter of 2015 and the first half of 2016.

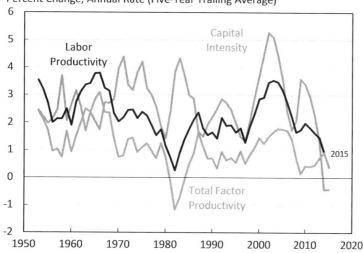

Figure 12
Labor Productivity and Major Components, 1950–2015
Percent Change, Annual Rate (Five-Year Trailing Average)

All of the G-7 countries except Canada saw appreciable slowing in their rates of capital deepening between 1994-2004 and 2004-2014, as shown in Figure 13a. Like in the United States, this slowdown in capital deepening was even larger than the slowdown in TFP growth in Germany, Japan and the United Kingdom. In contrast, France and Italy have seen larger slowdowns in TFP growth than in capital deepening, as shown in Figure 13b.

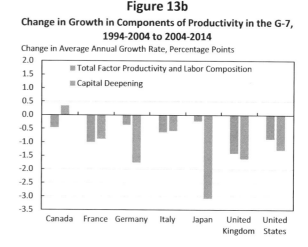

Figure 13a
Capital Deepening in the G-7
Percent Change in Capital Intensity, Annual Rate

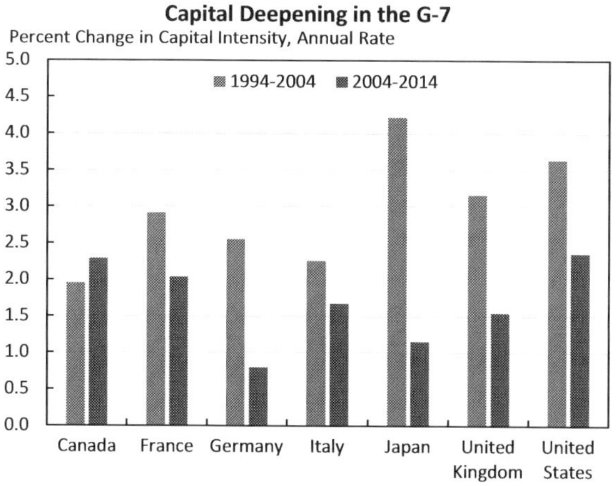

Figure 13b
Change in Growth in Components of Productivity in the G-7, 1994-2004 to 2004-2014
Change in Average Annual Growth Rate, Percentage Points

13

If the productivity slowdown were caused primarily by low rates of investment, it may provide an encouraging signal for the future outlook. It would demonstrate that the economy has not fallen short on innovative ideas or moved towards secular stagnation, but instead just needs more investment. Moreover, the lack of investment is not a complete mystery. Accelerator models of investment—where growth in investment depends on the change of the growth rate in output—can explain much of the slowdown. In a 2014 analysis, the IMF finds that since the global financial crisis, low or negative growth in the profitability of private investment may be a key factor depressing investment in advanced economies (IMF 2014). The world economy has simply not grown fast enough to generate rapid investment growth.

The global nature of this problem is important. In a globalized economy, many firms will invest based on global demand. Low expectations for that demand pull down investment in all major economies, which feeds into slower growth again. Not only do we have policy tools to help push towards higher investment, but to some degree such investment slowdowns have historically been self-correcting: investment tends to be negatively serially correlated, with investment busts followed by booms and vice versa. In the United States TFP is essentially unrelated to its past values, while capital deepening is negatively serially correlated.

The Role of Slowing Total Factor Productivity Growth: Supply Causes Demand

Slowing total factor productivity growth has, however, also played a role in all of the G-7 economies. There is some evidence that the recent slowing in a range of economies began before the crisis, around 2004, as much of the low-hanging fruit from the information technology revolution was deployed throughout advanced economies. From this perspective, a creeping slowdown on the supply side of the economy in the run-up to the crisis could have led to a slowdown in income growth, such that growing levels of debt on the consumer side collided with a slowdown in output growth. Debt overhang among households may have resulted in pessimism, weighing on consumer spending and business investment. In addition, the expectation of slower productivity growth, and the slower wage growth associated with it, have potentially played a role in the post-crisis dynamics of consumption and investment as well.

In Japan's case, though, the slowdown in productivity growth goes back much further. Japan saw rapid productivity growth in the second half of the 20th century as its productivity approached that of the United States and other advanced economies, converging from under 20 percent of U.S. output per hour in 1950 to 69 percent in 1997, as shown in Figure 14. But since then, Japan's relative productivity has plateaued and fallen slightly to 64 percent of the output per hour of U.S. workers, the lowest of any G-7 economy.

Figure 14
G-7 Productivity (Output per Hour)

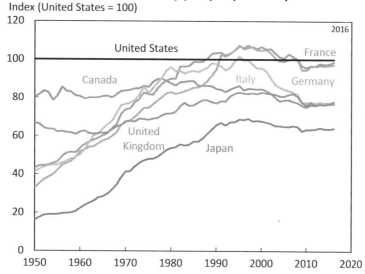

Two factors, in particular, have played a role in the relative stagnation of Japan's productivity growth: the demographic transition towards an older population and the shift towards the service sector, which has lower productivity growth than the manufacturing sector. Both of these are more acute versions of challenges that other economies have faced and, at least in the case of demography, will continue to face.

The Demographic Transition. As Figure 15 shows, the major advanced economies all face the challenge of aging populations, though this challenge is particularly acute in Japan. Research by James Feyrer (2007) has found that changes in the age structure of the labor force are correlated with changes in labor productivity. Workers are generally at their most productive in middle age, so as demographic changes have led to a shrinking share of these workers in their prime years, aggregate productivity has slowed. Feyrer's results suggest the aging of the workforce will place downward pressure on TFP growth for decades to come. Recent research on the United States finds that a 10-percent increase in the fraction of the population over 60 is associated with a 5.5-percent drop in the growth rate of GDP per capita over ten years, with two-thirds of the slowdown due to reduced productivity growth and the remainder due to lower labor force growth (Maestas, Mullen, and Powell 2016).

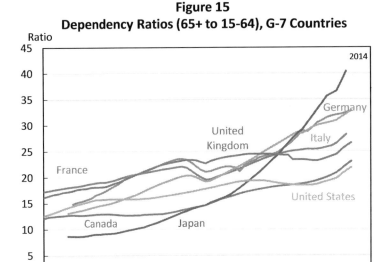

Figure 15
Dependency Ratios (65+ to 15-64), G-7 Countries

Demographics competed with other factors in the United States and Japan following World War II. In both countries, investment and technological progress were able to overcome the TFP slump due to demographics. Recent work by Claudia Goldin (2016) suggests that people are now healthier in old age and working longer. Findings like these and the success of retraining programs focused on boosting productivity and labor force attachment among older workers like Germany's (Berg et al. 2015) suggest that the changing nature of health and longevity can intersect with policy to counteract slowdowns in productivity growth that would be expected based solely on links between demography and productivity found in historical data.

The Services Transition. The share of services in employment, consumption, and value added is rising in all of the advanced economies—although it is still considerably lower in Japan and the euro area, where services make up just over 70 percent of both employment and value added, than in the United States, where services represent about 80 percent of both employment and value added. This shift is in part the result of the increased demand for services relative to durable goods by a more affluent and older population.

This transition creates a headwind for productivity growth because in virtually all economies, productivity growth is faster in manufacturing than in services. There are many reasons service-sector productivity growth could be slower. In some sectors, human interaction may be difficult to replace, making capital or technology less of a factor in increasing production. In others, quality gains may simply be hard to measure. The OECD (2015) has also suggested that technology diffuses less easily between frontier firms and other firms in the services sector compared to manufacturing.

But the fact that in Japan, especially, productivity growth in services has been so much lower than productivity growth in manufacturing is indicative that more is going on than just technology. Japan has consistently had the largest gap between productivity in manufacturing and productivity in services of any of the major advanced economies, and in the last decade it has had the fastest productivity growth rate in manufacturing of any of the G-7 economies. It is also one of only two countries that has had negative measured productivity growth in services in the last decade, as shown in Figure 16. This discrepancy suggests an ongoing challenge for overall productivity growth as the Japanese economy continues to shift towards services.

Figure 16
Average Annual Growth of Labor Productivity by Sector, 2004-2014

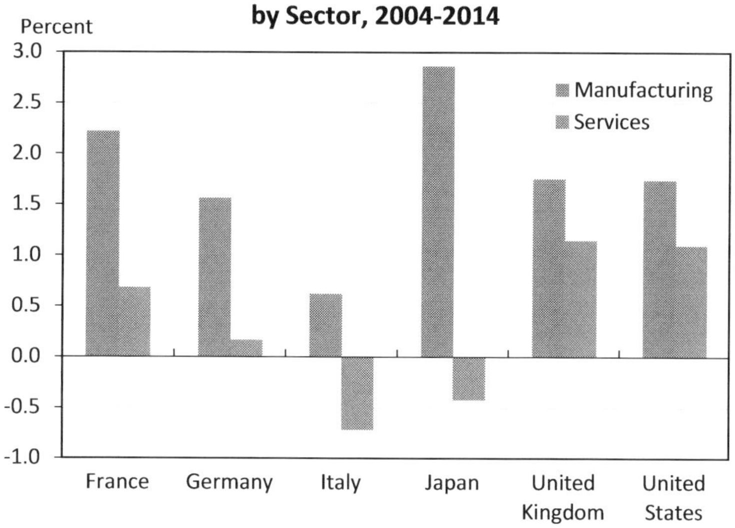

A number of different explanations have been put forward for the particularly slow growth of productivity in Japan's service sector. Some observers (*e.g.* OECD 2008) have noted that while Japan has exposed its manufacturing sector to the rigors of global competition for decades as part of its postwar industrial policy, it has sheltered its domestic service sector, reducing incentives to increase efficiency. Hoshi and Kashyap (2011) have argued that the government has made more progress on reducing regulation in manufacturing than in services, where a range of rules constrain growth in retail and wholesale trade, real estate, finance, and hospitality. Some (*e.g.* Smith 2015) have suggested that the persistence of the *shūshin koyō* lifetime employment system enjoyed by part of the labor force, which prevents companies from firing workers or adjusting their pay fluidly to match their productivity or labor market conditions, reduces efficiency in labor-intensive sectors. Kyoji Fukao and other researchers (2014) have pointed to the increased role of part-time workers and slow investment in information technology among possible reasons for sluggish productivity growth in Japan. The Abe Administration's renewed focus on reducing red tape, streamlining relevant legal and tax codes for key service industries, and helping small and medium-sized enterprises to adopt modern technologies is likely to help address Japan's particular challenges in this space.

The Labor Force

GDP growth depends on the increase in productivity (or output per hour) and the increase in hours. The growth of hours depends on demographic facts about the age structure of the population, on the rate of immigration, and on the labor force participation rate. In practice, policy can and does affect all three of these: for example, a number of countries have deliberately taken steps to encourage births and to expand immigration. But I will focus particularly on the third factor, labor force participation, because this can, by itself, help offset some of the challenges associated with demography, including in Japan where the population is actually shrinking. Moreover, as I have just discussed, such steps may also contribute to stronger productivity growth.

As the population ages in advanced economies, an increasingly large fraction of the population has retired, driving down the labor force participation rate. Japan has been experiencing a decline in the labor force participation rate since 1992, while the U.S. labor force participation rate peaked in 2000, as shown in Figure 17. In the wake of the Great Recession, the participation rate in the United States and many other advanced economies has also faced downward cyclical pressure, but this has largely if not entirely abated in the United States.

Figure 17
Labor Force Participation Rate, 1975-2015

The larger issue has been the longer-run trends. Up until 2000, the dominant trend in the United States was the large-scale entry of women into the workforce, which outweighed a continued decline in participation by men. By 2000, however, women's entrance into the U.S. workforce ended, and since then they have largely followed the downward trend that men had been on starting decades earlier. In contrast, Japan has seen considerably less erosion in the labor force participation rate for men and has seen a steady increase for women—to the point where prime-age women's labor force participation in Japan—that is, participation by women between the ages of 25 and 54—slightly exceeds that in the United States, as shown in Figure 18.

Figure 18
Prime-Age Labor Force Participation, Japan and United States

The Abe Administration's package of efforts—including encouraging the involvement of women in corporate and municipal management positions, increasing accessibility and quality of childcare and nursery school, improving the conditions of maternity leave, and making workplaces more flexible—have helped continue and extend these trends. This comprehensive strategy will hopefully pay off for years to come in terms of boosting female labor force participation, setting an example for the United States and countries around the world that family issues should be a core part of economic policy.

At the Council of Economic Advisers (CEA) we have been focused on understanding the decline in the labor force participation rate in the United States, both in historical and comparative perspective. I want to share some of that thinking with you, both because it is applicable to both Japan and the United States and because I believe it has broader implications for some of the more simplistic, traditional recommendations about structural reforms in labor markets.

The U.S. Challenge of Falling Participation by Prime-Age Workers: The Importance of Demand

The decline in the percentage of prime-age adults participating in the U.S. labor market is not unique to this economic recovery. Instead, it is the continuation of a troubling pattern in labor force participation going back for more than a half-century for men and about fifteen years for women. In 1953, 97 percent of prime-age men were in the labor force. Today, the fraction stands at just 89 percent (Figure 19a). Meanwhile, 74 percent of prime-age women are participating in the labor force today, compared to 77 percent in 1999 (Figure 19b). These trends are troubling in part because of decades of research on the human toll of involuntary joblessness, including its effects on life satisfaction, self-esteem, and physical health and mortality.

Figure 19a
Prime-Age Male Participation Rate, United States

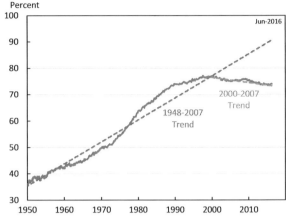

Figure 19b
Prime-Age Female Participation Rate, United States

A recent CEA report focuses on the decline in participation for prime-age men, largely because participation for this group has been decreasing for longer than it has for prime-age women, and thus more data are available to understand some of this decline's underlying causes (CEA 2016b). The decrease in the percentage of prime-age men in the workforce does not appear to be primarily caused by a reduction in labor supply. By and large, it is not highly educated men who have left the labor force, but those with a high school education or less. The decrease in participation is also not explained by increasing reliance on working spouses—in fact, men who are out of the labor force are increasingly unlikely to be married—or by increases in disability insurance enrollment.

The most important evidence suggests that shifts in labor demand are more responsible for the decline in prime-age male participation than shifts in labor supply. While men with a high-school education have seen their participation decrease sharply, they have also seen their relative wages fall—from over 80 percent of annual wages for workers with a college degree or more in 1975 to less than 60 percent in 2014. This decrease in both employment and wages suggests that the demand curve has shifted (or has shifted even more than the supply curve has shifted): reductions in the desire to employ less-skilled workers have simultaneously reduced their employment *and* lowered their wages. While the source of this decline in demand is not readily apparent, a number of possibilities exist: technological change and globalization (which have led to a decline in manufacturing employment), skill-biased technological change, and the massive increase in recent decades of formerly imprisoned Americans (who may face lower demand for their labor) are just a few.

Many of these changes in demand, like the increased demand for skilled labor and the reduced share of manufacturing jobs, are common across a wide range of countries. But at least using available data from around 1980 to 2010, the United States ended up with both a larger decline in prime-age male labor force participation and also a larger increase in inequality than nearly any OECD member country. This suggests that demand is not destiny, and that how shifts in demand interact with institutions is also important.

The U.S. Experience in Comparative Context

The United States ranks near the bottom of the OECD in terms of the percentage of prime age men and women in the workforce, as shown in Figure 20a and Figure 20b. But since 1990, the United States has also seen a sharper decline in the prime-age male labor force participation rate than all but one OECD economy and, unlike the vast majority of OECD countries like Japan, has seen prime-age female labor force participation fall slightly.

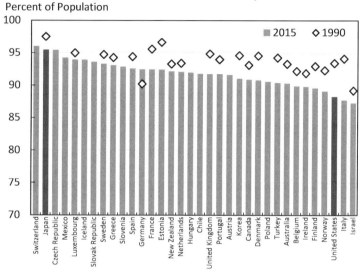

Figure 20a
Prime-Age Male Labor Force Participation Rate

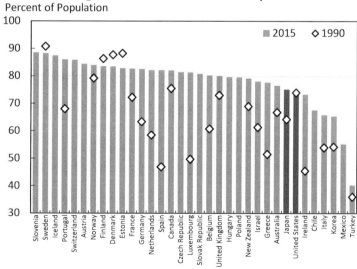

Figure 20b
Prime-Age Female Labor Force Participation Rate

The weak position of the United States relative to the rest of the industrialized world in terms of labor force participation has persisted even though the United States has the least overall labor market regulation, the least employment protection, and the second-lowest minimum cost of labor relative to other OECD countries, as shown in Table 1. Japan's labor market is also well above the median for the OECD by these metrics, although it is not as flexible as the U.S. labor market.

Table 1
OECD *Going for Growth* Indicators

	Percentile Rank (100 = Most Flexible/Most Supportive)	
	United States	Japan
Measures of Labor Market Flexibility		
Overall Labor Market Regulation (2014)	100	91
Employment Protection for Regular Employment (2013)	100	80
Minimum Cost of Labor (2014)	96	92
Coverage of Collective Bargaining Agreements (2013)	94	82
Measures of Institutional Labor Market Support		
Expenditure on Active Labor Market Policies per Unemployed (2013)	6	39
Net Childcare Costs, Couples (2012)	10	33
Implicit Tax on Returning to Work, Second Earner (2012)	10	67

At least part of a plausible answer about the difference between the experience of the United States and other countries is that government support for the U.S. labor market is less than that of other countries. The United States spends 0.1 percent of GDP on active labor market policies, like job search assistance and job training, which help people find work and retool for new jobs. This is less than Japan's 0.2 percent of GDP and the OECD average of 0.6 percent of GDP—and less than any other OECD country except Chile and Mexico.

A number of features of the U.S. labor market particularly discourage women's participation in the workforce, given that women usually bear a disproportionate burden of childcare and housework. The United States is the only OECD country not to guarantee paid leave, either for illness or for family reasons (such as maternity or paternity leave). And while the gross cost of U.S. childcare is about average for the OECD, subsidies for childcare in the United States are considerably below the OECD average, making the net cost of childcare among the most expensive of any advanced economy. Moreover, while the United States generally has low tax rates, our tax system imposes a relatively high tax wedge between primary and secondary earners on average.

At the very least, the differences in labor force participation between the United States and other OECD countries with more supportive labor markets suggests that the United States may have something to learn when it comes to creating conditions for meaningful employment—and that the standard view among economists about the tradeoffs between flexibility and support likely misses at least part of the story. Part of Japan's success in boosting the female labor force participation rate under the Abe Administration may be directly related to efforts to address childcare costs, implicit tax penalties on second earners in married couples, and the availability of childcare, as well as issues in the working environment for women.

My main takeaway from all of this is that the answers on labor markets are considerably more complex and nuanced than any simple, ideologically conventional answer—and many policies either do not entail these tradeoffs at all or can be designed to minimize them. In this respect, the efforts by the Abe Administration to increase participation, particularly among women, represent welcome steps forward—steps from which the United States can learn quite a bit.

The Policy Agenda

The United States and Japan have both recovered and exceeded our pre-crisis economic peaks. We both have low unemployment rates. But we also face varying degrees of short-run challenges, including faltering growth and consistently low inflation in Japan. At the same time, we both face varying degrees of long-run challenges—including productivity, where growth has slowed in both countries but is especially slow in Japan, as well as falling labor force participation and high levels of inequality, both of which are major challenges for the United States.

I have argued that many of these issues are interrelated. Weak aggregate demand in the short run translates into less investment and thus less productivity growth in the long run. Adverse demographic trends—particularly in Japan—are a headwind not just to labor force growth but also potentially to productivity growth. And some of the forces that have increased inequality may also have had an adverse effect on growth.

The substantial variation in all of these outcomes across countries proves that none of these challenges are inevitable and that we can learn from each other's policy choices about how to promote robust growth that is sustained, sustainable, and broadly shared. The specifics, of course, differ from country to country but I want to list eleven broad areas that are applicable in varying degrees to the United States, Japan, and other advanced economies.

(1) Expanding aggregate demand. As I have discussed, aggregate demand plays an important role in the short-run trajectory of the economy in terms of bringing about full employment, maximum output, and inflation levels that make economies more resilient in the future. But it also, through an accelerator mechanism, increases the incentive for business investment and thus helps increase future productivity growth.

(2) Expanding trade. Expanding trade would not just yield static gains grounded in comparative advantage. It would also have the potential to increase innovation through a range of channels, including learning by exporting, greater specialization in innovative activities, access to larger markets by high-productivity firms, and expanded competition. That is why President Obama is pushing for Congress to pass TPP and has also prioritized negotiations on the Transatlantic Trade and Investment Partnership (TTIP) with the European Union. Japan learned long ago that the competition and large scale of the global marketplace can lead to world-class innovation. A high-quality trade agreement that protects worker rights and the environment, as well as intellectual property, the TPP will create incentives and tools to help firms boost productivity, while setting the rules of the road for fair trade in the Asia-Pacific region for decades to come. TPP is also carefully designed to help small and medium-sized businesses access export markets, helping ensure that its benefits are widely shared.

(3) Increasing public investment. Additional public investment in primary research and human capital (see below) is critical to productivity growth. In the United States, additional public investment in infrastructure is crucial both to productivity growth and to increasing demand that will help bolster labor force participation. Some of the voluminous evidence we have for the importance of infrastructure comes from Japan, where Andrew Bernard, Andreas Moxnes, and Yukiko Saito (2015) find that firm performance increased near new stations when Japan extended the *shinkansen* high-speed railway south in 2004. The boost came largely from expanded business relationships with suppliers in other locations. But the experience of Japan and many other countries also cautions that it is important to ensure that infrastructure funding is invested wisely and that research funding focuses on the basic research that has the largest spillovers and thus is most likely to be undersupplied by the market. In the United States, we have recently enacted a five-year investment of $306 billion in surface transportation, a roughly 5 percent increase in real terms, and have proposed substantial new investments focused on green infrastructure that build on this base.

(4) Strengthening education and training. Education plays a critical role in productivity growth, labor force participation, and inequality. In the United States we have focused on everything from making pre-school education universal, to improving K-12 education and making sure all students are offered a computer science course, to making college more affordable and getting students better information about college completion and the quality of colleges. I also would note the Abe Administration's commitment to equipping the workforce with the skills necessary in the high-tech economy, and its focus on expanding access to high-quality pre-school programs.

(5) Reforming the tax system. Japan had long had the highest corporate tax rate in the world but beginning in 2012 has cut the rate so that it now stands below 30 percent, a move that will hopefully provide additional incentives for domestic investment. Japan has also reduced property taxes on small and medium-sized enterprises to help encourage their growth. This leaves the United States with the highest corporate tax rate of any advanced economy—but at the same time, we do not collect a commensurate amount of revenue. Moreover, our international tax system is broken, imposing distortions on corporate decision making while collecting relatively little revenue. Cutting the top statutory corporate tax rate, expanding and reforming the tax base, reducing the preference for debt-financed investment, and establishing a minimum tax that ensures some taxation of foreign earnings, as President Obama has proposed, would all help U.S. productivity growth while potentially also reducing financial fragility.

(6) Reducing the medium- and long-run deficit. Almost all of the advanced economies have fiscal gaps going forward. Many of these economies have fiscal space in the short run. Moreover, much of the fiscal challenge in most countries is related to the composition of spending and taxes. But acting on the medium- and long-run deficit would be a welcome way to ensure sustainability and further bolster fiscal space. In the United States, we have taken steps on both the revenue and spending side that have helped reduce the fiscal gap to less than 2 percent of GDP and have proposed to close the remainder of the gap with a balanced combination of revenue achieved through a progressive broadening of the tax base and reduced spending on entitlements largely through the reform of the health system. Steps to reduce the medium- and long-run fiscal gap in Japan are even more important.

(7) Fostering technology. Technology is particularly important for productivity growth and higher wages and depends on everything from basic research to building out the wired and wireless infrastructure that deliver the Internet. To that end, the Obama Administration has taken a wide range of steps, including reforming the patent system; increasing spectrum for mobile broadband while also experimenting with spectrum sharing; helping to increase R&D to nearly 3 percent of GDP; expanding competition in key sectors; fostering a light-touch, multi-stakeholder approach to key issues like privacy and cybersecurity; and investing in expanded access for connectivity, especially in schools, low-income areas, and rural areas. Japan already has an impressive record of extending connectivity through broadband and cellular networks. Yet some (*e.g.* Kushida 2011) have argued that Japan's domestic regulatory policies at times have impeded the emergence or full exploitation of innovation. Advances like the large-scale deregulation of the energy sector last April will help in this regard.

(8) Increasing competition and making sensible regulatory reforms. Competition is essential to productivity growth, and there is evidence, at least in the United States, that competition has eroded over time. In Japan, lack of domestic competition in certain sectors, in many cases maintained by regulation, has long held back productivity growth even as competition in external sectors has helped move productivity growth in the opposite direction. Promoting competition is not just a matter of antitrust enforcement but also depends on a range of other policies to remove barriers to entry. In the United States, some of these obstacles include barriers to workers changing occupations and restrictions on land use. In Japan, liberalizing the energy sector and the agricultural distribution system, as well as liberalization in health care and other services industries, are likely to provide a boost to productivity in these sectors and possibly spillovers to other industries as well. In addition, capital—especially for small businesses—remains a major challenge.

(9) Increasing labor force participation. A number of the policies I have been describing would help boost labor force participation. A focus on more flexible workplaces, support for childcare, reforms in the taxation of secondary earners, and active labor market policies that support job search can all play a role as well.

(10) Boosting wages. A number of the policies I have described would also help boost wages, in many cases by boosting productivity growth. But direct steps to help ensure that workers are receiving the benefits of a growing economy are also necessary. In the United States we are pushing to raise the minimum wage, something that 18 States and the District of Columbia have done in recent years. Expanded unionization and more worker voice would also help improve the bargaining power of labor in the United States, boosting wages and reducing inequality. Putting the recommended minimum wage on an upward path in Japan will hopefully help put upward pressure on wages economy-wide. Moreover, continued pressures on nominal wages through the Tripartite Commission and other mechanisms may be helpful, although, to date, they proved somewhat challenging in practice. In addition, weakening the duality between the lifetime employment system and non-regular workers in Japan may help increase churn in the labor market, increasing productivity by helping firms find more productive matches and helping workers bargain for higher wages with competing offers.

(11) Expanding immigration. Finally, last but not at all least is expanding immigration. While this has many dimensions that go beyond economic policy and is a choice that different countries have to make for themselves, I would note that the single largest economic impact of any policy proposed by President Obama comes from comprehensive immigration reform, which CBO estimated would add 3.3 percent to real GDP after a decade. Notably, this increase would come not just from a larger workforce but also from expanded TFP, as immigrants bring new ideas and foster more ideas from native workers as well—as evidenced by the fact that, according to a study by the Partnership for a New American Economy, immigrants or the children of immigrants founded more than 40 percent of Fortune 500 companies, including Google, eBay, Sun Microsystems, and Intel (PNAE 2011). In this area, the Abe Administration is taking a more welcoming stance toward foreign-born workers.

Notes to Figures and Tables

Figure 1
Source: International Monetary Fund, *World Economic Outlook.*

Figure 2
Note: Data for Japan and euro area through 2016:Q1.Population data for euro area are quarterly interpolations of annual data.
Source: National sources via Haver Analytics; CEA calculations.

Figure 3
Source: National sources via Haver Analytics.

Figure 4
Source: National sources via Bloomberg Professional Service.

Figure 5
Source: International Monetary Fund, *Japan: Selected Issues* (July 2016).

Figure 6
Note: Fiscal expansion calculated as the difference between the primary fiscal balance in the reference year and its value in 2007. Asterisks (*) indicate projections.
Source: International Monetary Fund, *Fiscal Monitor* (April 2016).

Figure 7
Notes: Data for 2013 and 2014 are provisional estimates.
Source: Organisation for Economic Co-operation and Development.

Figure 8
Source: National sources via Haver Analytics.

Figure 9
Source: Organisation for Economic Co-operation and Development.

Figure 10
Source: Conference Board, Total Economy Database; CEA calculations.

Figure 11
Note: The figure shows the deviation of investment between 2008 and 2014 from forecasts made in the spring of 2007. Black diamonds indicate the average percent deviation of total investment. Colored segments show the contribution of the components of investment—business, residential, and public—to the deviation. Public-sector contributions to residential and nonresidential investment are excluded from these categories when data for these contributions are available. Peripheral Euro Area category includes Greece, Ireland, Italy, Portugal, and Spain. Core Euro Area category includes Austria, Estonia, Finland, France, Germany, Latvia, Luxembourg, Malta, the Netherlands, Slovakia, and Slovenia.

Source: International Monetary Fund, Fiscal Monitor Database; Consensus Economics; national sources via Haver Analytics.

Figure 12
Source: U.S. Bureau of Labor Statistics, Productivity and Costs; CEA calculations.

Figures 13a and 13b
Source: Organisation for Economic Co-operation and Development; CEA calculations.

Figure 14
Source: Conference Board, Total Economy Database; CEA calculations.

Figure 15
Source: Organisation for Economic Co-operation and Development; CEA calculations.

Figure 16
Source: Organisation for Economic Co-operation and Development; CEA calculations.

Figure 17
Source: U.S. Bureau of Labor Statistics, Current Population Survey; Statistics Bureau, Japan Ministry of Internal Affairs and Communications, Labor Force Survey; CEA calculations.

Figure 18
Source: U.S. Bureau of Labor Statistics, Current Population Survey; Statistics Bureau, Japan Ministry of Internal Affairs and Communications, Labor Force Survey; CEA calculations.

Figures 19a and 19b
Source: U.S. Bureau of Labor Statistics, Current Population Survey; CEA calculations.

Figures 20a and 20b
Source: Organisation for Economic Co-operation and Development; CEA calculations.

Table 1
Source: Organisation for Economic Co-operation and Development, *Going for Growth* 2016; CEA calculations.

References

Berg, Peter B., Mary K. Hamman, Matthew M. Piszczek, and Christopher J. Ruhm. 2015. "The Relationship between Establishment Training and the Retention of Older Workers: Evidence from Germany." NBER Working Paper No. 21746.

Bernard, Andrew B., Andreas Moxnes, and Yukiko U. Saito. 2015. "Production Networks, Geography, and Firm Performance." NBER Working Paper No. 21082.

Council of Economic Advisers (CEA). 2016a. "Chapter 1: Inclusive Growth in the United States." *Economic Report of the President.*

_____. 2016b. "The Long-Term Decline in Prime-Age Male Labor Force Participation." Report.

DeLong, J. Bradford and Lawrence H. Summers. 2012. "Fiscal Policy in a Depressed Economy." *Brookings Papers on Economic Activity* 44 (1): 233-297.

Eggertsson, Gauti B., Neil R. Mehrotra, Sanjay R. Singh, and Lawrence H. Summers. 2016. "A Contagious Malady? Open Economy Dimensions of Secular Stagnation." NBER Working Paper No. 22299.

Feyrer, James. 2007. "Demographics and Productivity." *Review of Economics and Statistics* 89 (1): 100-109.

Furman, Jason. 2015. "It Could Have Happened Here: The Policy Response That Helped Prevent a Second Great Depression." Remarks at Macroeconomic Advisers Washington Policy Seminar.

Furman, Jason and Peter Orszag. 2015. "A Firm-Level Perspective on the Role of Rents in the Rise in Inequality." Presentation at "A Just Society" Centennial Event in Honor of Joseph Stiglitz, Columbia University.

Fukao, Kyoji, Kenta Ikeuchi, YoungGak Kim, HyeogUg Kwon, Tatsuji Makino, and Miho Takizawa. 2014. "The Structural Causes of Japan's Lost Decades." Working paper.

Goldin, Claudia. 2016. "How Japan and the US Can Reduce the Stress of Aging." NBER Working Paper No. 22445.

Hoshi, Takeo and Anil Kashyap. 2011. "Why Did Japan Stop Growing?" National Institute for Research Advancement report.

International Monetary Fund (IMF). 2014. "Chapter 3: Perspectives on Global Real Interest Rates." *World Economic Outlook*, April 2014.

_____. 2016a. *Acting Now, Acting Together: Fiscal Monitor, April 2016*. Report.

_____. 2016b. "_World Economic Outlook Update:_ Uncertainty in the Aftermath of the U.K. Referendum." Report.

Kushida, Kenji E. 2011. "Leading without Followers: How Politics and Market Dynamics Trapped Innovations in Japan's Domestic 'Galapagos' Telecommunications Sector." _Journal of Industry, Competition and Trade_ 11 (3): 279-307.

Maestas, Nicole, Kathleen J. Mullen, and David Powell. 2016. "The Effect of Population Aging on Economic Growth, the Labor Force, and Productivity." NBER Working Paper No. 22452.

Mourougane, Annabelle, Jarmila Botev, Jean-Marc Fournier, Nigel Pain, and Elena Rusticelli. 2016. "What is the Scope for Public Investment to Lift Long-Term Growth?" OECD Ecoscope Blog. June 3.

Organisation for Economic Co-operation and Development (OECD). 2008. _OECD Economic Surveys: Japan 2008._ Paris: OECD Publishing.

_____. 2015. _The Future of Productivity_. Report.

_____. 2016. _Going for Growth 2016_. Report.

Ostry, Jonathan D., Atish R. Ghosh, and Raphael Espinoza. 2015. "When Should Public Debt Be Reduced?" IMF Staff Discussion Note.

Partnership for a New American Economy (PNAE). 2011. "The 'New American' Fortune 500." Report.

Smith, Noah. 2015. "Japan's Productivity Puzzle." Bloomberg View. June 29.

World Wealth and Income Database. 2016. "The World Wealth and Income Database." Alvaredo, Facundo, Anthony B. Atkinson, Thomas Piketty, Emmanuel Saez, and Gabriel Zucman. Accessed July 27, 2016.

Made in the USA
Middletown, DE
29 July 2023

35941682R00018